Mammoth and Mastodon

by Jennifer Zeiger

CHERRY LAKE PUBLISHING * ANN ARBOR, MICHIGAN

Published in the United States of America by Cherry Lake Publishing
Ann Arbor, Michigan
www.cherrylakepublishing.com

Content Adviser: Gregory M. Erickson, PhD, Paleontologist, Department of Biological Science, Florida State University, Tallahassee, Florida

Reading Adviser: Marla Conn, Read With Me Now

Photo Credits: Cover, © Michael Rosskothen/Shutterstock.com; page 4, © Catmando/Shutterstock.com; page 6, © Darryl Brooks/Dreamstime.com; page 8, © David Steele/Shutterstock.com; page 10, © Sean Pavone/Dreamstime.com; page 12, © Morphart Creation/Shutterstock.com; page 14, © Ozja/Shutterstock.com; page 16, © Ryan M. Bolton/Shutterstock.com; page 18, © Vladislav Gajic/Shutterstock.com; © Mikekwok/Dreamstime.com.

LIBRARY OF CONGRESS CATALOGING-IN-PUBLICATION DATA

Zeiger, Jennifer, author.
  Mammoth and mastodon / by Jennifer Zeiger.
      pages cm.—(Dinosaurs) (21st century junior library)
  Summary: "Learn all about the ancient animals known as mammoths and mastodons, from how they lived to how they are related to today's elephants."—Provided by publisher.
  Audience: K to grade 3
  Includes bibliographical references and index.
  ISBN 978-1-63362-383-5 (lib. bdg.)—ISBN 978-1-63362-411-5 (pbk.)—ISBN 978-1-63362-439-9 (pdf)—ISBN 978-1-63362-467-2 (e-book)
  1. Mammoths—Juvenile literature. 2. Mastodons—Juvenile literature. 3. Extinct mammals—Juvenile literature. 4. Animals, Fossil—Juvenile literature. [1. Prehistoric animals.] I. Title.
QE882.P8Z45 2016
569.67—dc23   2014045656

Cherry Lake Publishing would like to acknowledge the work of
The Partnership for 21st Century Skills.
Please visit www.p21.org *for more information.*

Printed in the United States of America
Corporate Graphics
July 2015

CONTENTS

A woolly mammoth had a thick coat of woolly hair.

What Were Mammoths and Mastodons?

Picture a group of **prehistoric** elephants. They are covered in thick hair. The hair is long and woolly. The animals munch on grass in a wide field. These are mammoths. Miles away is another furry elephant. It lumbers alone through a thick forest. This is a mastodon. Both of these ancient animals were related to the elephants we know today.

Mammoths and mastodons had mostly died out by about 10,000 years ago.

The earliest mastodons lived about 25 million years ago. Mammoths first appeared about 5 million years ago. Both animals lived for millions of years. Early humans even hunted them for a time. There are no mastodons or mammoths living today, though. They are **extinct**.

Ask Questions!

We know that humans met mammoths and mastodons. But how do we know? Talk to a parent, teacher, or librarian. Ask them to help you find more information. Check in books or search online. What can you find out?

Mammoths and mastodonos were similar to their modern elephant relatives.

What Did Mammoths and Mastodons Look Like?

The word *mammoth* can be used to describe something big. And these animals were really big! In fact, mammoths were named for being so large. Most mammoths were about the size of today's elephants. Mastodons were just a little shorter.

A mammoth's tusks were longer than a mastodon's. Some tusks were so long that they curved over each other.

Mammoths and mastodons looked a lot like elephants. They had large heads and wide, flat ears. They also had very long noses called trunks. Two big teeth called tusks stuck out of their mouths. These animals had large, heavy bodies. Four thick, strong legs supported them.

Create!

Mammoths and mastodons did not look exactly alike. Look up pictures of both in books or online. Now draw your own mammoth and mastodon. Label the ways they are different from each other.

Mammoths needed a warm coat of hair in their wintery world.

Elephants today do not have much hair. But their prehistoric relatives were very hairy. The hair ranged from yellowish brown to reddish brown. Northern mammoths and mastodons had the thickest hair. When these animals lived, the weather was much colder than it is today. The thick hair kept them warm.

Mammoths lived in open areas without many trees.

How Did Mammoths and Mastodons Live?

Mammoths and mastodons lived across North America and Central America. They were also found in Asia, Europe, and Africa. These two animals lived in very different **habitats**. Mammoths usually lived in open **grasslands**. Mastodons were more often found in forests.

A mastodon's teeth were more pointed than a mammoth's.

Mammoths mostly ate grass. This food was easy to find in grasslands. Mammoths had wide, **ridged** teeth. These ground up the food the mammoth chewed. In the forests, mastodons found trees and shrubs to eat. A mastodon's cone-shaped teeth could cut and chew tough twigs and leaves. Its tusks could also scrape off bark to eat.

Visitors can see mammoth bones in
many museums.

The bones of many mammoths are often found together. This leads experts to believe that mammoths lived in **herds**. This is also how elephants live today. Mastodon bones are usually found alone. Some experts think these animals lived on their own.

This baby mammoth lived tens of thousands
of years ago.

We learn about mammoths and mastodons in many ways. One way is from **fossils**. People have also found whole bodies frozen in ice. These animals even appear in cave paintings. People drew these pictures thousands of years ago. But we still do not know everything. There is always more to learn about these ancient animals!

Look!

Look up some pictures of cave paintings. Ask an adult to help you find the best ones. What shapes, animals, and other objects are in the paintings? Do you see anything surprising?

GLOSSARY

extinct (ek-STINGKT) describing a type of plant or animal that has completely died out

fossils (FAH-suhlz) the preserved remains of living things from thousands or millions of years ago

grasslands (GRAS-landz) large, open areas of grass

habitats (HAB-i-tats) places where animals are usually found

herds (HURDZ) large groups of animals that stay together or move together

prehistoric (pree-his-TOR-ik) belonging to a time before history was recorded in written form

ridged (RIJD) having narrow, raised strips on the surface

FIND OUT MORE

BOOKS

Higgins, Melissa. *Woolly Mammoths*. North Mankato, MN: Capstone Press, 2015.

Morrison, Taylor. *The Great Unknown*. Boston: Houghton Mifflin, 2001.

Wheeler, Lisa. *Mammoths on the Move*. Orlando, FL: Harcourt, 2006.

WEB SITES

The Field Museum— Mammoths and Mastodons: Titans of the Ice Age

http://archive.fieldmuseum.org /mammoths/?_ga=1.57952298 .1424295012.1412201159

Check out images of these ancient animals, and learn about one baby mammoth that was discovered in the ice of Siberia.

Wisconsin Historical Society—The Mammoth Mystery

www.wisconsinhistory.org/kids /mammoth/main.html

Follow clues to help a scientist solve the mystery surrounding a mammoth in Wisconsin.

INDEX

ABOUT THE AUTHOR

Jennifer Zeiger lives in Chicago, Illinois. She writes and edits children's books on all sorts of topics.